ALMOST
an EVENING

D1557608

ETHAN COEN

——

ALMOST
an EVENING

THREE RIVERS PRESS
NEW YORK

Copyright © 2009 by Ethan Coen

Published in the United States by Three Rivers Press, an imprint of the
Crown Publishing Group, a division of Random House, Inc., New York.
www.crownpublishing.com

THREE RIVERS PRESS and the Tugboat design are registered trademarks of
Random House, Inc.

World Premiere
Presented By
Atlantic Theatre Company
New York City, 2008

Library of Congress Cataloging-in-Publication Data

Coen, Ethan.
Almost an evening / Ethan Coen. — 1st ed.
1. Hell—Drama. 2. Future life —Drama. I. Title.
PS3553.O348A78 2009
812'.54—dc22   2008051748

ISBN 978-0-307-46041-7

Printed in the United States of America

Design by Lauren Dong

10 9 8 7 6 5 4 3 2 1

First Edition

Contents

Foreword

Upon these one-acts' first performance I heard a parting theatergoer complain it had been "not even almost an evening." I considered making that the title of the published scripts, but on reflection it seemed wrong. Wrong, first, to give the published plays a title different from that under which they had been performed. Wrong, second, to push self-deprecation so far it sounds like self-censure. I take *some* pride in my work, and together these plays *do* make up almost an evening—I don't care what anyone says.

—*Ethan Coen*

Almost an Evening was first performed at Atlantic Theater Company's Stage 2 in New York City on January 22, 2008. The following cast was directed by Neil Pepe:

WAITING

NELSON	Joey Slotnick
RECEPTIONIST	Mary McCann
MR. SEBATACHECK	Jordan Lage
McMARTIN	Mark Linn-Baker
POLHEMUS	Del Pentecost

FOUR BENCHES

ONE	Jonathan Cake
EARL	Del Pentecost
MR. BOODRUM	J. R. Horne
CONTROL	F. Murray Abraham
TEXAN	Jordan Lage

DEBATE

GOD WHO JUDGES	F. Murray Abraham
GOD WHO LOVES	Mark Linn-Baker
ANGEL ONE	Del Pentecost
ANGEL TWO/UNDERSTUDY	J. R. Horne
YOUNG WOMAN	Mary McCann
YOUNG MAN	Jordan Lage
MAITRE D'	Jonathan Cake
WAITER	Joey Slotnick
LADY FRIEND	Elizabeth Marvel

WAITING

A drab waiting room.
Mr. Nelson, in a suit, sits waiting.
A high counter separates him from a receptionist who sits with
  her back to us. She types.
And types.
Mr. Nelson clears his throat.
He glances at his watch.
He looks around, reaches into his jacket.
Without looking up from her typing (nor will she ever):

RECEPTIONIST: No smoking.

Nelson's hand freezes, then slowly emerges from his jacket,
  empty.
He looks around.
He looks at his watch.
He glances down at the side table next to him, picks up the two
  magazines displayed there, looks from one to the other.

NELSON: Are there any other magazines?

RECEPTIONIST: No.

He looks at the first magazine.

NELSON: *Highlights for Children.*

The receptionist continues typing.
He looks at the second magazine.

NELSON: *U.S. News & World Report.*

The receptionist continues typing.
He squints at the second magazine.

NELSON: Last April.

The receptionist yanks the sheet out of her typewriter. She
briefly proofs it against a laminated reference sheet before
inserting a new piece of paper and resuming typing.
Mr. Nelson puts down the magazines.
He looks around.
He rises and heads for a small pebbled glass window down-
stage.

RECEPTIONIST: It's sealed.

He freezes.
He slowly turns and goes back to his chair.
He drums his fingers.
He looks around. This time, however, as he faces the fourth
wall, something dawns on him.
He stares.
Alarmed, he looks all around.
He looks suspiciously at the receptionist.

NELSON: There's something funny about this room, isn't there?

RECEPTIONIST: Yes.

He waits for her to continue.
She only types.
He elaborates:

NELSON: There's no door.

RECEPTIONIST: No.

He nods.

NELSON: So—how did . . .

He thinks.
Again, something dawns. He smiles and, nodding comprehen-
sion, bounces a pointing finger at the receptionist.

NELSON: I'm dead, aren't I?

RECEPTIONIST: Yes.

He nods, pleased to have figured it out.
He looks at the room again with new appreciation.

NELSON: So this is hell.

RECEPTIONIST: No.

Taken aback, he picks up the two magazines and looks from
one to the other.

NELSON: *Heaven?*

RECEPTIONIST: No.

He puts down the magazines, puzzled.

NELSON: So . . . it's a sort of . . . purgatory.

RECEPTIONIST: Sort of.

NELSON: So . . . it's not eternal.

RECEPTIONIST: No. Damn!

She stops typing, rolls the paper up a couple of lines, shakes some Wite-Out, paints it onto the paper, blows on it.

NELSON: So . . . how long do I spend in here?

RECEPTIONIST: Eight hundred and twenty-two years.

She rolls the paper down and resumes typing.
Again Mr. Nelson looks around, trying to imagine it.

NELSON: And only you to talk to.

RECEPTIONIST: I don't talk.

He chuckles.

NELSON: But that's a . . . what do you call it? When it contradicts itself?

RECEPTIONIST: I can answer questions for six more minutes. After the first ten minutes, I only type.

He laughs.

NELSON: Oh come on! I've been here more than four minutes!

She types.
His smile evaporates.
He looks at his watch.
He looks around.
He looks at the receptionist.

NELSON: Eight hundred and *how* many y—

RECEPTIONIST: Twenty-two.

He nods. He shakes his head. He sucks a tooth, thinking.

NELSON: What if I have to make pee-pee?

RECEPTIONIST: You won't.

He nods thoughtfully.
He looks down at the side table.

NELSON: Do they ever change the magazines?

The receptionist gives a short humorless hoot.
Mr. Nelson nods. He looks around.

NELSON: Well eventually—I mean, once I've served my time—
how . . .

He nods at the fourth wall.

NELSON: How do I get out?

RECEPTIONIST: After seven hundred and fifty years, they put a
door in.

He stares at the fourth wall, trying to picture it.
He stares for quite a while.
The receptionist types on.

* * *

A plain office. A man sits behind a desk, writing.
He writes for a while.
There is a knock.

MAN: Yes?

The door opens hesitantly.

MAN: Yes, come in.

> *Mr. Nelson enters, still wearing the same suit, clutching a piece of paper.*
> *The writing man rises and extends his hand.*

MAN: Mr. Nelson? I'm Mr. Sebatacheck.

> *Nelson beams.*

NELSON: Hello.

SEBATACHECK: Have a seat.

NELSON: Thank you. Thank you, Mr. Sebatacheck.

SEBATACHECK: The typist, where you were waiting, when you left did she give you a . . .

NELSON: Yes!

> *Nelson holds up the piece of paper.*

SEBATACHECK: May I?

NELSON: Yes, yes!

> *He hands it across.*

SEBATACHECK: Great.

> *Sebatacheck keeps up a line of banter as he carefully checks Nelson's paper against a plastic-laminated reference sheet. His speech is directed down at his desk as he busily refers between Nelson's paper and his master sheet.*

SEBATACHECK: Well, I'll bet you've had enough of *that* place.

Still beaming, Nelson shakes his head.

NELSON: Boy! Phooph!

SEBATACHECK: Ready for heaven then?

NELSON: Boy! I've been ready for . . .

He shakes his head.

SEBATACHECK: Ready for quite a number of years, I would think.

NELSON: Boy!

SEBATACHECK: Some folks say the first few years are the toughest. Although I don't suppose it ever really . . .

NELSON: Mm-mm. No sir.

SEBATACHECK: But then, you'll like heaven. Everybody does—well, listen to me!

He chuckles at himself, still checking the paperwork.

SEBATACHECK: Talk about stating the obvious!

Nelson laughs along with him.

SEBATACHECK: Okay, let me just . . . what?—no!

He squints at Nelson's paper, his smile gone.

SEBATACHECK: No!

He shakes his head, then laughs with disbelief.
Alarmed, Nelson looks from the paper to Sebatacheck.
Sebatacheck sits back in his chair, laughing and shaking his head.

SEBATACHECK: No no no no no! Achh.

Still smiling and shaking his head, he makes a helpless gesture at the paper. He enunciates carefully at Nelson:

SEBATACHECK: Eight *thousand* and twenty-two years.

* * *

The waiting room again.
The receptionist types.
Nelson sits in his chair, bitterly jabbing a finger toward her.

NELSON: Eight hundred and twenty-two years. You sat RIGHT there. That's right, lady. I'm talking to you. You sat RIGHT there and you said Eight hundred and twenty-two years. I asked you to REPEAT it. You said it TWICE. Eight hundred and twenty-two years. I'm talking to you, lady. YOU. Miss busy-screwing-up-somebody-else's-inforMAtion. You think I don't remember? You think just because it was a few thousand years ago I don't remember? What did I, confuse it with something else you said in the last six thousand five hundred years? You think maybe I got CONFUSED with all the amusing chitter-chatter SPEWING out of your mouth? And let me tell you something else, lady. You think I'm not gonna tell them about you? About how YOU screwed up? About how you gave me WRONG information? . . . That's right, lady. You type. You type while they LET you type. A position of TRUST. A position of AUTHORITY. Important DOCUMENTS. And you. YOU. Mental MIDGET. Sure. You type. Enjoy it while you can, lady . . . Heeyeah!

* * *

The office again.
A different man, McMartin, sits behind the desk.
On the desk are two sheets of paper, Nelson's report and the
laminated reference page.
Nelson sits in front of the desk but is sprawled forward, elbows
resting on the desktop, one hand holding a business card up
toward McMartin.
Nelson is sobbing.
He sobs for some time, motionless, displaying the card.
McMartin helplessly shakes his head. Finally he turns two
palms up.

MCMARTIN: I don't even know why they brought you here.

Nelson brings the words out between hacking sobs:

NELSON: Because . . . I've waited . . . eight thousand . . . and twenty-two . . . *years!*

MCMARTIN: I understand.

NELSON: Eight thousand . . . and twenty-two . . . *years!*

MCMARTIN: Yes. I understand. But, Mr. Nelson—your term is *twenty*-eight thousand and twenty-two years.

NELSON: That's not . . . what Mr. . . . *Sebatacheck* said!

MCMARTIN: I don't understand how he could possibly—

NELSON: He *checked* it! He *triple* checked it! I *begged* him to, because I didn't think it could be *that* long! He guaran*teed* me it was right!

McMartin: I don't understand how he could—

Nelson: He said he'd *be* here when I came back! Or if he wasn't, he said he could be *reached*! Mr. *Sebatacheck*! He *swore* to me! He gave me his *card*!

McMartin: There's no way he could've—

Nelson: *Please* take it! *Please* take it! Mr. *Sebatacheck*!

McMartin sighs. He leans forward and takes the card.

Nelson: Mr. *Sebatacheck*!

McMartin looks at the card. Dubiously shaking his head, he drags the phone across his desk.
It is a rotary phone. Referring to the card, McMartin slowly . . . dials . . . seven . . . digits.
After a beat he dials . . . four . . . more . . . digits.
He leans back for a long listening wait.
Suddenly:

McMartin: Mr. Sebatacheck, please . . . Mr. McMartin, in admissions . . . I see . . . I see . . . I see.

He hangs up.
He looks thoughtfully at Nelson.
He draws a deep breath.

McMartin: Since Mr. Sebatacheck cannot be reached, I'm afraid I have no choice but to—

Nelson: *Why?!* *Why* can't he be reached?

McMartin: —I'm afraid you'll have to serve out the balance of your term.

NELSON: Mr. *Sebatacheck*!

McMARTIN: Your term is *twenty*-eight thousand and twenty-two years. I—

NELSON: *He* said *eight* thousand! *Why* can't he be reached?

McMartin draws another deep breath.

McMARTIN: Mr. Sebatacheck has passed away.

Nelson stares, stunned.

NELSON: Puh—

He laughs, incredulously.

NELSON: Passed away?! That's not . . . how could . . . Passed a*way*?!

He rises, laughing hysterically.
He slams the back of one hand into the palm of the other to further stress the two stressed syllables:

NELSON: *That's* ab*surd!*

* * *

The waiting room.
Nelson sits waiting in the same chair. He stares straight ahead.
The receptionist types.
The tableau holds for some time.

* * *

The office again.

Nelson hovers anxiously over the shoulder of a new man, Pol-
hemus, who refers back and forth between Nelson's report
and the laminated plastic reference sheet.
Nelson agitatedly waves another paper.

NELSON: And this is a notarized affidavit I had McMartin sign, *guaranteeing* that I could leave after twenty-eight thousand and twenty-two years. And I had him specify there, you'll notice I had him specify—

POLHEMUS: Yeah.

NELSON: —I had him specify it was not just on his own author-ity but by authority of, and binding upon, management, its agents, its nominees and assigns—

POLHEMUS: Yeah yeah.

NELSON: —in perpetuity, so that—

POLHEMUS: Acchhh.

He disgustedly flips down his pencil and leans back.

NELSON: —so that . . . what?

Polhemus shakes his head.

NELSON: *What?*

Polhemus grimaces.

POLHEMUS: McMartin really screwed this up.

For a moment Nelson is afraid to speak.

NELSON: . . . What do you mean? What're you trying to say? What're you—

He hops up and down, waving the paper.

NELSON: This *guarantees* that I—

POLHEMUS: Yes yes, you're getting out.

Nelson stares.

POLHEMUS: You should have gotten out a long time ago.

Nelson stares.

POLHEMUS: You were right. You were supposed to serve *eight* thousand and twenty-two years.

Nelson stares.

NELSON: I . . . You . . .

POLHEMUS: I don't know what McMartin was looking at.

NELSON: He . . . You mean I . . . spent twenty thousand extra—

POLHEMUS: I'm sorry.

NELSON: I spent the last twenty thousand years—

POLHEMUS: I'm very sorry. He'll catch hell for this, you can be sure of that.

Shaking his head at the paper, Polhemus grimaces and hisses:

POLHEMUS: Nitwit.

Nelson is staring vaguely off.
He looks at Polhemus.

NELSON: But now I'm free to go.

Polhemus shrugs a why-not:

POLHEMUS: Sure.

Nelson hesitates.

NELSON: To heaven.

POLHEMUS: Yeah. As a matter of fact . . .

He consults his watch.

POLHEMUS: Jesus. You better hurry.

NELSON: Huh?

POLHEMUS: The shuttle. It leaves in two minutes.

NELSON: Right. Okay. Is Mr. McMartin nearby—if I could have
just a moment with him—

POLHEMUS: For God's sake let it go man, you've only got two
minutes! Let it go! The shuttle only leaves once every ten years!

NELSON: Every ten—WHERE DO I GO?

Polhemus drags the phone over and starts dialing as Nelson
skips frantically toward the door.

POLHEMUS: To your left, down the hall—you'll see signs—

As Nelson exits Polhemus calls out, over the painfully slow
click-click-click-click-click of the rotary phone:

POLHEMUS: —I'll try to reach 'em, get 'em to wait—

* * *

The waiting room.
The receptionist types.
Nelson sits staring glassily into space.
He drones:

NELSON: I-i-i-i-i-i-i-i-i-i-i-i-i-i-i-i-i-i-i-i-i-i-i-i-i-i-i-i-i-
fffffff . . .

A suspense beat through which Nelson stares at nothing.

Then he launches into song:

NELSON: . . . *one* of those bottles should happen to fall . . .

He hesitates. He squints at a point in space, trying to remem-
ber his place in the song.

* * *

The office.
Mr. Sebatacheck, the first admissions man, sits behind the
desk. He is relaxed, leaning back, feet up, reading a maga-
zine, occasionally plucking a grape from a bunch that rests
on a paper towel on his desk.
There is a soft, slow knock.
In an absent sing-song, his eyes still on the magazine:

SEBATACHECK: Ye-es.

The door slowly opens.

Nelson, clutching a sheet of paper, takes a shuffling step in, turns, closes the door behind him, turns again, and shuffles into the office. He is an abject, beaten man, his voice hollow, his manner pathetic:

NELSON: Okay. Can I go now?

SEBATACHECK: Excuse me?

Sebatacheck's eyes slide lazily off the magazine and, resting on Nelson, grow puzzled.
Nelson is slowly raising his report.

NELSON: Can I go to heaven now? Here's my re—

Nelson's eyes widen. He gasps.

NELSON: Mr . . . Sebatacheck!

Sebatacheck is still puzzled.

SEBATACHECK: Yes?

NELSON: They said . . . they told me you were dead!

SEBATACHECK: I was *dead*? That's ab*surd*.

Nelson nods.

NELSON: That's what *I* said.

SEBATACHECK: What do you have there?

Zombielike, Nelson extends the paper.

NELSON: My paperwork.

Still puzzled, and a little irritated, Sebatacheck takes the paper and looks between it and Nelson throughout Nelson's forlorn narrative:

NELSON: I don't think there should be any problem now. Last time, after I missed the shuttle, I lost my—

SEBATACHECK: The shuttle?

NELSON: To heaven. I lost my temper because it meant spending an extra ten years in the waiting room, so they—

SEBATACHECK: *Extra* ten years?

NELSON: Ten more years, til the next shuttle. But I'd already waited the first eight hundred and twenty-two years; and then seven thousand two hundred more when it turned out I was supposed to serve eight *thousand* and twenty-two years— that's when I met you, Mr. Sebatacheck—and then an extra twenty thousand years just because of a stupid mistake that Mr. McMartin made, so the extra ten years made me lose my temper. And then they told me I wasn't *allowed* to lose my temper and I'd have to serve an extra ninety-nine thousand years for cursing. So, yes, I cursed some more but then I stopped, and I haven't cursed once in ninety-eight thousand four hundred and forty-nine years.

Sebatacheck gazes at him for a beat.

SEBATACHECK: I bet that's a record.

NELSON: So now I've been in purgatory for a hundred and twenty-seven thousand and thirty-two years—

SEBATACHECK: Purga—

Something hits Sebatacheck and forces out a laugh.

NELSON: . . . and I'm awfully tired of it so if there aren't any other problems, can I go to heaven now?

SEBATACHECK: Purgatory . . .

He is lost in reminiscence. Nelson prods:

NELSON: I don't mind if I have to sit at a tram stop for a year or two.

SEBATACHECK: I'm sorry. I just realized—you're from before Disclosure.

NELSON: Huh?

Sebatacheck wears a smile of nostalgia.

SEBATACHECK: Jesus. I'd forgotten how we used to . . .

NELSON: Disclosure?

SEBATACHECK: Yeah, they decided to stop kidding people. We tell them up front now.

NELSON: Tell them?

SEBATACHECK: That they're in hell.

Nelson can't quite take this in.

NELSON: *Who* is.

SEBATACHECK: You are. You people.

Nelson solemnly shakes his head.

NELSON: No, I've been in purgatory. I've been waiting to go to heaven. In the waiting room.

Sebatacheck shakes his head. His speech is patient, a little too loud, and meticulously enunciated, as if Nelson were a dull child.

SEBATACHECK: We were pulling your leg. We were teasing. You *stay* here.

NELSON: . . . Teasing?

SEBATACHECK: Yes. False hope. But we've stopped doing that. We stopped a long time ago.

NELSON: So . . . When am I going to heaven?

SEBATACHECK: You're not *going* to heaven. We were just pretending. But now we're telling people. They've decided that despair is more effective, so now we tell people. You're in hell. It's eternal.

NELSON: So . . . I'm staying.

SEBATACHECK: That's right. Forever. We *tell* people now—less fun for us; more effective for you people.

NELSON: I see.

SEBATACHECK: It's more effective that way.

NELSON: I see.

SEBATACHECK: After Disclosure they cut us back. Couldn't string people along if we wanted to. Don't have the manpower.

NELSON: I see.

SEBATACHECK: Okay?

NELSON: Okay. I see. Thank you.

> *He stands there, nodding.*
> *At length Mr. Sebatacheck holds up the paperwork between two fingers.*

SEBATACHECK: Do you want this back? Or should I drop it in the trash?

> *Nelson thinks.*

NELSON: You can drop it in the trash. Thank you.

SEBATACHECK: Okay.

> *He leans forward and does so, then goes back to his magazine. Nelson nods, slowly turns, but then stops and turns back.*

NELSON: So . . . you've been okay, then?

SEBATACHECK: I've been fine. Thank you.

> *Nelson nods, for a good beat.*

NELSON: I see.

> *He turns and shuffles toward the door. He stops and turns back with another thought.*

NELSON: Is that a new magazine?

Eyes on the magazine, Sebatacheck goes back to his sing-song voice:

SEBATACHECK: Yes it i–is.

Nelson hesitates.

NELSON: . . . Can I borrow it?

Sebatacheck rolls his eyes, drops the magazine on his chest, and smiles thinly at Nelson.

SEBATACHECK: You know better than that, Mr. Nelson.

NELSON: Yes. I see.

SEBATACHECK: . . . Okay?

NELSON: Okay.

Nelson shuffles to the door, opens it—

NELSON: Okay.

—and shuffles out, closing the door behind him.
A beat.
Sebatacheck licks a finger, turns the page.
A thought sets him chuckling:

SEBATACHECK: . . . Ninety-nine thousand years . . . for cursing . . .

He shakes his head, smiling; his smile fades as he continues to read.

FOUR BENCHES

_____

In black until noted.

We hear a swinging door being pushed open and, on release, flapping back and forth. Padding footsteps end in the creaking of wood as someone sits. The saloon-style door continues to flap in diminishing intervals until, at length, it shudders into silence.

A beat.

The first voice we hear is British-accented; the second, American—specifically, Texan.

ONE: . . . Well?

TWO: . . . Huh?

ONE: *Well?*

TWO: . . . What?

ONE: Well? Any luck?

TWO: . . . Sorry, I'm not sure I—

ONE: Potts?

TWO: . . . *Potts?*

ONE: Oh. I'm sorry, I . . . I thought—

Two: No, I—sorry friend, I ain't—

One: Sorry. Terribly sorry. Can't see a thing.

Two: Yeah.

One: Can't see my hand in front of my face.

Two: Yeah, plenty dark.

One: Mm. Dark indeed.

Two: Yeah. *(beat)* What happened?

One: *(guarded)* . . . When?

Two: The lights—why aren't they—

One: Oh! *(beat)* Power.

Two: Oh. *(beat)* But . . . the lights are *on.*

One: I beg your pardon?

Two: Outside. The lights outside.

One: . . . Are on.

Two: Heck yeah.

One: Hm. *(beat, then indifferently)* A mystery, then.

Two: . . . You tried the switch?

One: Switch?

Two: Light switch?

ONE: . . . *Is* there one?

Wood creaks.

TWO: Well shoot, I . . . I as*sume*.

Lights on.
Plank walls and floor, a long wooden bench, steam.
Sitting on the bench is a man in a conservative suit, shirt but-
toned to the neck, severely knotted tie, bowler hat. Propped
next to him are a furled umbrella and a briefcase. The
other man, paunchy and middle-aged, stands with his
hand at the light switch. Except for a large white cowboy
hat, he is naked. After a beat just long enough for the
tableau to register, the clothed man sucks in his breath and
shrieks.

TWO: *(naked)* I, uh . . .

The clothed One grabs his briefcase and clenches it, white-
knuckled, before his face.

ONE: Turn it off!

TWO: Jeez, I, uh . . .

ONE: Off! Now!

The lights go off as Two complies. Again in darkness:

ONE: Thank you.

TWO: Well sure, I . . .

ONE: Thank you. I'm sorry. Must seem odd.

TWO: Aww, I understand. You're English.

ONE: . . . Pardon?

TWO: See, round here we'll mostly steam nekkid.

ONE: Um . . .

TWO: Local norm.

ONE: *(sigh)* To be sure. But I'm not here for the sauna, actually. I'd arranged a meeting, and—because it was meant to be private, it just, it just, it wouldn't do, your seeing my face; you shouldn't even be here, whoever you are. —You didn't, did you?

TWO: Huh?

ONE: See my face?

TWO: No no.

ONE: Awkward if you had. You're not involved. Best keep it that way. Secret identities, so on. We love our little secrets.

TWO: Oh sure . . . Sure, I get it . . .

ONE: Mm.

TWO: It's like . . . a spy thing?

ONE: *(guarded)* . . . What is?

TWO: Whatever.

ONE: . . . Mm. Yes. Something like that.

TWO: So—should I leave?

ONE: Leave?

Two: Yeah, you want me outta your hair?

One: . . . Nnnnnooo, better stay, at this point, I should think. Leaving now you might see the other gentleman on his way in. See his . . . his face.

Two: Uh.

One: Awkward. For the other gentleman.

Two: Potts?

One: *(sigh; beat)* Potts.

Two: So you want me to just . . . wait here?

One: If it's not terribly inconvenient.

Two: No. Hell no. Came in for a steam, I'll have a steam.

One: Mm.

Two: . . . Spy thing, uh?

One: Something like that.

Two: Kind of a James Bond kind of a . . .

One: *(chuckles)* Oh, nothing quite that exciting, I'm afraid.

Beat.

Two: Steamed here before?

One: Not steamed. Been.

Beat.

Two: There a rack?

One: . . . Rack?

Two: Hat rack?

One: Um . . .

Two: Neb mind.

   Beat.

Two: You sure you want me here while you talk to Potts?

One: *(taken aback)* What? *God* no.

Two: Well you got me waiting here—

One: *(politesse recovered)* No no, I—no, sorry, I was thinking once Mr. Potts did arrive, perhaps you'd be kind enough to leave at that juncture.

Two: Oh.

One: Leaving us to our little talk.

Two: Uh-huh.

One: Having seen neither of us.

Two: Yeah, I get it.

One: Mm.

Two: . . . Yeah, okay.

ONE: Thanks so much. Saves an awkwardness.

TWO: Yeah, sure.

ONE: Mm. But how—if you don't mind my asking?

TWO: Go right ahead.

ONE: How did you manage to slip by the man downstairs?

TWO: Man?

ONE: Security.

TWO: *(beat)* Security?

ONE: *(longer beat)* Oh dear.

> *We hear the door crash open. We hear bellowing under the ACK-ACK-ACK of automatic-weapon fire and, in its strobe, we see the naked man flail.*
> *The firing ends and, in the restored darkness, the jingling of ejected casings peters out.*
> *Quiet.*
> *Then—a cry in which despair and self-loathing mingle:*

ONE: Aaaahh . . .

* * *

> *In black, twittering birds.*

VOICE: You the, uh . . . ?

ONE: Yes. You're . . .

Lights up on a park bench. Near it is a garbage can marked
TRASH.

Sitting upon the bench is One, the British steam-bather.
Standing before him is a small elderly man whose yoked
shirt, buttoned to the neck, sits loosely on a wizened
turkey-buzzard frame. His eyes, in thick black-framed
eyeglasses, bug out from a wrinkly, whispy-haired head.

ONE: . . . Mr. Boodrum?

The old man sits.

OLD MAN: I just wanted to look atcha. I just wanted to see the
last man seen my Earl.

ONE: Sir, though I realize there is nothing I could possibly say—
sir, I would like, however feebly, to attempt to convey to you
how profoundly sorry we are that your son became . . . became . . .

OLD MAN: I s'pose, to you, it's a game. Not a game, exactly: all
in a day's work.

ONE: Sir, I assure you—

OLD MAN: A face, to you. A body.

ONE: Sir, I—

OLD MAN: An innocent bystander. A run-over armadilla.

ONE: Sir, I did not have the pleasure of—though we spoke,
briefly, your son and I, I did not have the pleasure of—

OLD MAN: Earl was a colossus.

Beat.

OLD MAN: Earl had his own fam'ly. Three boys. And the little girl. Dominique. A colossus.

Beat.

OLD MAN: You know why he was in New York?

ONE: To be honoured . . . I was told.

OLD MAN: They miss their Daddy. And I miss my Earl.

ONE: Sir, I assure you—

OLD MAN: Yeah, that's right. Employee of the Year. Ran a feedlot, down Denton. For a large aggibidnes. We was plenty proud.

ONE: Indeed.

OLD MAN: They said it was reasons a national security.

ONE: Sir?

OLD MAN: Said no arrests. Perpetrators believed to have fled the country. Mmm. Fled it. Couldn't muster any details, they said. Reasons a national security. That's what they said.

ONE: Yes sir, and I too have certain limits as to—

OLD MAN: But I told 'em, well, I want to talk to someone who was there. Y'owe it to me.

ONE: Yes sir.

OLD MAN: It's my right. Earl's death, why, it ain't gonna be just papered over. "National security"—why, that's paper. This was a human thing. This man was a colossus. For *you*, maybe, it's a paper thing.

ONE: No sir. Quite the contrary. In fact, Her Majesty herself asked me to convey to you—

OLD MAN: Her *Majesty?*

ONE: Yes sir, she personally asked me—

OLD MAN: Son, we fought a revolutionary conflict, we stained this soil with patriots' blood, so that we would not have to call *no* one Her Majesty.

ONE: Uh . . .

OLD MAN: So that we would not have to bend our knee to *no* earthly bein'.

ONE: Yes sir.

OLD MAN: So let's not talk about any Majesty.

ONE: Yes sir.

OLD MAN: . . . I don't mean to get all scratchy about it, son. But ya see, in my book, Earl, he's away up here *(indicating with a raised hand)*, and her majesty, she's away down here. So her proclamations and so forth, why they ain't gonna console me none.

ONE: I understand, sir.

OLD MAN: And that goes for Earl's family, and forever body in Denton.

ONE: Yes sir.

   Long beat.

OLD MAN: *(sudden and loud)* Well?

One starts.

ONE: . . . Sir, I . . . I've tried to express—

OLD MAN: You ain't said one feelin' word, sonny. You can do better'n that. Why, every word you've said, it could a been engraved on a card.

Beat.

OLD MAN: A store-bought card.

Beat.

OLD MAN: With her majesty's seal.

ONE: . . . Sir . . . in my own poor way—

OLD MAN: Course, I been monopolizin'.

Beat.

ONE: Sir—

OLD MAN: I'm lookin' at your face.

ONE: . . . Sir?

OLD MAN: I'm lookin' at your face, son, and I feel sad.

The abashed Brit tries to hold his gaze.

OLD MAN: I feel sad that the last face Earl gazed upon, it had so little sympathy. Earl was a warm man. A people person.

Beat.

OLD MAN: You ain't no people person.

One bows his head.

OLD MAN: They flew me up. Though I offered to fly at my own expense.

Beat.

OLD MAN: Earl was a big man. Not just physically.

Beat.

OLD MAN: And he was my boy.

Beat.

ONE: . . . Sir . . .

Fade out.

* * *

In black, twittering birds—but different-sounding than in the foregoing.

ONE: Yes, quitting!

VOICE: Steady.

ONE: Quitting!

Lights up on a park bench. Near it is a garbage can marked RUBBISH.

*Control, an older man, sits on the bench. He holds a rolled-up
newspaper. An agitated One paces. Binoculars swing from
a strap round his neck.*

ONE: It's a horrible business!

CONTROL: Steady.

ONE: Oh!

CONTROL: It was his . . .

ONE: Father, yes.

CONTROL: Mm.

ONE: I felt such an ass!

CONTROL: No, no.

ONE: What's the point! We shuffle papers, we, we, we deal in
abstract concepts, we, and then someone dies, somebody
bloody up and dies and we, it's not even somebody in the
game, it's—I don't know *where* Potts was—and there's,
there's, we just go on about our business as if *that* had mean-
ing, as if, as if—

CONTROL: Steady on.

ONE: —as if *that* had importance, when we can't even find the
words, in simple human contact, cannot for the life of us find
one word, one single meaningful feeling word, so where's
the—you tell me—where's the—oh!

CONTROL: Yes. I see.

ONE: One heartfelt word. So what do our plans, our concepts . . .

CONTROL: Yes yes. I see.

ONE: *(pleading)* Do you?

CONTROL: Mm . . .

Control nods in silence. Then he leans back, fist to his lips, head contemplatively cocked, studying his charge. A lengthy inhale draws his head away from his fist: he has a thought:

CONTROL: Did you tell him that Her Majesty herself—

ONE: Oh!

CONTROL: . . . Mm.

He nods again. Another beat.

CONTROL: . . . Suggestion: Let it percolate.

ONE: What?

CONTROL: Simmer.

ONE: What?

CONTROL: Percolate. Your decision.

ONE: What? What? No. No no no, I'm out.

CONTROL: Mm . . .

He nods.

CONTROL: Question: Why?

ONE: Good God man, I've just been telling you—

CONTROL: *(suddenly animated)* These principles, these principles, these abstract—which you dismiss—rather *blithely*
dismiss—if these prin—

> *He stops, suddenly and for no apparent reason. After a beat of*
> *staring into space he becomes keenly interested in the finger-*
> *nails of one hand. One, who has stopped pacing, raises his*
> *binoculars and, standing motionless, examines the horizon*
> *upstage, one hand clenched behind his back. After a beat a*
> *young woman enters right. She is pushing a pram. One*
> *wheel rhythmically squeaks as she unhurriedly crosses the*
> *stage. She exits left.*
> *Control unfreezes.*

CONTROL: —if these abstract principles mean nothing to you—
question: if, say, *Hitler*, had—

ONE: Please!

CONTROL: No-no! *Hitler*—suppose he'd—

ONE: Good God, man—

CONTROL: If *Hitler*, or, say, this fellow Gad*d*afi—

ONE: Listen to yourself!

CONTROL: Yes but people's lives are at stake! Merely because you
don't see them, because they're abstract, you—

> *He winces and whips open his newspaper and affects to read.*
> *One again studies the view, hand clenched behind his*

back. A child bounces in from stage left on a pogo stick. He advances midway across the stage and then bounces energetically more or less in place, facing the audience.

After a great deal of bouncing, One's discipline cracks: his head turns, hesitantly at first, to look back at the source of the noise.

At length Control too looks up from his paper, trying to cover his irritation with a smile:

CONTROL: . . . Look here, little fellow, why don't you *fuck off*?!

The child continues to bounce, smiling broadly. Control scowls at him.

Slow fade.

* * *

In black, creaking wood as someone rises, followed by padding footsteps and the push of a swinging door. The door flaps back and forth in diminishing intervals until, at length, it shudders into silence.

After a long beat, a sigh in which despair and self-loathing mingle:

ONE: Aaaahh . . .

Lights up on a new sauna. Same as the old except that a pair of longhorns is mounted just by the door.

Agent One sits wearing only a towel.

After another beat the swinging door opens. A middle-aged man enters wearing a towel and a cowboy hat. With one hand he stops the door from flapping behind him; with the other he takes off his hat and hangs it on one prong of the longhorns.

He sits.

One smiles and offers an ice-breaker:

ONE: I *won*dered what that was for.

TEXAN: . . . What.

ONE: That, uh . . .

> *The Texan looks at One, then at the longhorns, then stares at*
> *   One.*
> *Beat.*

TEXAN: Hats.

> *One nods, smiling.*
> *Beat.*

ONE: Just moved to Texas.

TEXAN: Mm? Likin' it?

ONE: Very much so. Too soon to say, but very much so.

TEXAN: Dandy.

ONE: It's part of a change I'm going through, a lifestyle change.

TEXAN: . . . That right.

ONE: Yes, my previous existence had become intolerable to me. The clandestineness, the furtive meetings, the sneaking around in sauna baths, the whispers, the lies. And of course I had no real friends, no intimacies, not really. Partly perhaps it was because I'm British—we do tend to be that way, the irony, the reserve, the *shield*, don't you see. And *heavens* I admire you people for your openness. Well, I began to think, why not share that openness! Become a people person! No longer hide behind civility and form! I thought, What a coward I've been, with my silly little secrets! And what a joy to give them up and, and fear no more, and *freeze* no more in this, this, this this arctic reserve! To tear open my heart! My warm and human heart! And show it! Oh yes, show it! To embrace people, because I'm ready now to embrace people—wonderful, wonderful people!—for the past is *not* prologue, it's *his*tory, and I'm ready to begin a new life that's warm and human and sweaty and real!

The Texan has been slowly straightening. He is now leaning back, hand on one knee and head cocked, staring at One.
One smiles at him.

ONE: Excuse me sir, but you remind me of someone, a wonderful man, a colossus, someone whom I also once met in a sauna bath. If you don't mind—tell me something about yourself, who you are, what you feel.

A long beat as the Texan stares.
One maintains his unnaturally broad smile.
At length the Texan stirs, gets to his feet with a creak of the bench, goes to the door, puts on his cowboy hat, straightens it, adjusts the curl of the brim, and exits.
One watches as the swinging door wobbles back and forth to final rest.
One looks front. After a long beat he emits a sigh in which despair and self-loathing mingle:

ONE: Aaaahh . . .

Beat.
Fade out.

DEBATE

In darkness, a voice:

VOICE: What do we call it?

> *The lights come up on a lectern center-stage. The man stand-*
> *ing behind it is rangy and weathered with long white hair*
> *and beard. Though older he is manly and vigorous. He*
> *wears a white robe, not immaculate, and sandals.*
> *Behind the lectern and to one side are two straightbacked*
> *chairs. Only one is occupied—by a well-groomed middle-*
> *aged man wearing a suit.*
> *For a long beat the man at the lectern gazes out at the audi-*
> *ence waiting for an answer. Finally he repeats his prompt:*

MAN: What do we call it? What do we call it? Anyone? What
do we call it we call it the Ten Commandments. Okay? Not
the Ten fucking Suggestions. They are a fucking moral *im-*
perative, you miserable sacks of shit. Now I want to see this
shit *observed.*

> *He lets this sink in and then starts to pace as the theme begins*
> *to animate him.*

MAN: Okay. And this imperative—let me just clarify here because I know there's been confusion—this is for *everybody,*
this is not just for the Jews. This is universal shit here, you

don't go, you know, Cayman Islands wherever, you know, when in Rome, oh I'll just covet the Roman neighbor's wife, *her* pussy doesn't count. Bull*shit*. That is relativistic horseshit. That is the Roman neighbor's wife's pussy fallacy and I call *bull*shit on that. I don't give a rat's ass where, Polynesia, they're topless, oh it's nature, they don't perceive it as sin, whatever, different cultures, the Eskimos have forty-seven words for snow—I don't *give* a shit. It applies to them too. This shit *applies*.

And this is not just some guy up here talking through his asshole. I hope you numbskulls have not forgotten who *decides* this shit. *You* don't decide this deep moral shit. Or when and where it applies. Are you kidding me—with your puny fucking brains? You don't know the state capitals and you're gonna decide this *moral* shit? No no. *I* decide, and I fucking *am* that am. So don't talk to me about the fucking Roman neighbor's wife. Dipshits.

Okay. Then there's the whining. I want less of the whining. I don't know why this pissing and moaning has gotten so bad lately, I mean we've always had *some* candybutts, but now it's *every*body. And it's worse in these cities here. You people going to shows, this is the kind of people where it's worst. So if the shoe fits. You know, "My parents were withholding. You weren't *there* for me. Daddy used to curse at me," all this crap. And not just You-ruined-my-life shit. Little things. Parking. Jesus fuck, *parking*. "Oh, it took us so long to park." You know, you sons of bitches used to *walk*. Or ride *asses*. And you're gonna drive a fucking *Lexus* here and bitch about having to spend ten minutes parking? Are you fucking shitting me? Okay, next time try riding an ass to the show. See how comfortable *that* is. See if you wanna bitch about finding a spot *then*, ya buncha fucking crybabies. Jesus fuck, maybe you'd like me to follow you through your whole cushy-ass life with a parking spot, kick it along after you like your suitcase on line at the airport. So you never have to drive around turning your head to the left and right. And maybe you want grapes dropped in your mouth, too, PITLESS, and the girls with the feather-fans, and maybe a little piece of velvet, maybe this big, you want it grazed back and forth across your buttocks very gently at all times to make you feel just exactly perfect. Is that fucking sufficient? You got nothing else to whine about now? Have I taken care of all your desires to your absolute total fucking satisfaction you kvetching little *shits*?

Okay, and then there's the weird shit. I don't even know what to call it but I think you all know what I'm talking about. So I want you to fucking cut it out. Like the body piercing. What in the name of god's fuck is *that*? Made in my image, right? And you're gonna what, put metal rings through it? This by you is an im*prove*ment? And through the lips, and the *nipples* now? I mean the *ears*, pierced *ears*, I didn't like it but I held my tongue. But *this*. And now through the *penis*, some of you people, and the *vulvas*? What next, hitting yourselves in the head with fishbats? You say, well, body piercing, it isn't forbidden—well, some shit I never told you not to because WHO'S GONNA DO THIS? Are you fucking nuts? I gotta tell you not to stick metal rings in your vulvas? What, for your car keys? You don't have POCK-ETS? This weird shit, I'm sorry, I'm lost. So let's just knock it off.

So there's that.

But *sin*—before I turn the floor over I gotta repeat, lest I leave the wrong impression—serious *sin*, this is still my main beef with you people—false God, neighbor's wife, et cetera. The other stuff—body piercing, huffing gasoline, betting on chicken fights—what are you doing? But that is *nothing* to this *sin* shit that you FUCKheads persist in pulling each and every GODDAMN DAY OF THE YEAR. Yeah. Some of you Shabbas even. Maybe I understand it more than the weird shit, yeah, but that is *not* permission. I *will* kick your fucking ass.

COUNT on it.

He seats himself. Now that his identity is established we may
call him God Who Judges. The man in the suit, whom we
shall call God Who Loves, rises to take his turn at the
lectern.

GOD WHO LOVES: Well. That's a, that's a hard act to follow. He
makes his points vividly, and with a great deal of salt. And I
respect that, and there is much to respect in what he says. But
let me put it all in a different context, if I may.

You are good people. You want to know how to live.
You're not experts in that. Some of you are doctors, lawyers,
academics, whatever, you have a certain area of expertise. But
here, in the big questions, you do not have expertise. You
have good common *sense,* but no expertise. And you feel like
you could use guidance.

These injunctions, the ones you've just heard, do they
help you? The threats, do they help you? Well, maybe some
of you, yes, that's what you need. Simple directions—that's
all you're after, and the rest, as they say, is just commentary.
But some of you—most of you, I think, attending a high-
class show such as this—need something else. Something
more. The reason you come to the theater, to shows like this
one, shows that tackle the big ideas, is that you are *not* cretins.
You don't need to be shouted at. You are interested in *ideas,*
and even when you don't know the answers, you still want to
take *intellectual responsibility* for yourselves. And moral responsibility. Because you are grown-ups. Not children to be
lectured to. Or yelled at. And when you need help—and
sometimes we all need help—well, you turn to something
higher.

You reach out. And this is beautiful. The quest itself is
beautiful. Because, you know, it ties us all to each other, each
to each. It makes you part of the community that seeks—not
after money! Not after status! Not that those things are evil,
but they aren't the *highest* things, and you—most of you—
recognize that. And *in* recognizing that, and *in* reaching out

for a loving guide, you come closer to each other. Because you reach for the same thing. Does that make sense?

I say again: it is the reaching out that is beautiful. You may not fully grasp. You may sometimes grasp wrongly. And sometimes there aren't, even, any final answers. But the Being to whom you reach loves you for reaching. Because you reach out. We all know it's hard to love someone who's closed-off, who's withdrawn. But someone who reaches out—the very act attracts love. So the desire for love is self-fulfilling: if you want it, it shall be there. Does that make sense? You only have to reach.

See, I'm not here to scold. I'm not here to lecture. I am here to love. I have been summoned by those of *you* who love. The others—well, you may not understand me. In some sense, you might not even hear me. That's okay. You didn't come for me. You came, maybe, to listen to *that* gentleman. Maybe you understand *Him*. And I repeat: that's okay. He isn't *wrong*. In his way, He too is beautiful. He's okay, that guy.

And before I turn the floor over, I just want to amplify that last thought. I know this event was billed as a debate, but I don't see it that way. I turn the floor over for rebuttal, but in fact I don't disagree with the gentleman. I don't expect you to *choose* between us. I don't want to be *right;* I don't want to show He's *wrong*. I want to reach you. And if *He* reaches you instead—okay, that's fine! In a sense, this isn't even about *us*. It's about *you*. And that you are interested enough in these matters to show up, to be here together, to listen, to reach— that's really what this is about. And that is beautiful.

Bless you all.

He seats himself. God Who Judges takes the lectern.
He stares down at the lectern for a long beat, organizing his
thoughts. When he finally speaks, his tone—at first, any-
way—is less truculent, more thoughtful, than during his
opening statement.

GOD WHO JUDGES: Well. I must say. A bigger crock of shit I have never heard.

I spoke earlier of the little piece of velvet that it sounded like some of you crybabies wanted drawn gently back and forth across your buttocks. Little velvet square, around yea big, I guess maybe I was thinking of those things you used to wipe across LPs. Get the lint off. Those of you who remember vinyl.

Well, what we've just seen here is a pandering DICK-WAD drawing a little velvet square back and forth across the buttocks of your brain. As it were. And it might feel good. I mean, that's the idea, to make you *feel* good. But of course it's all a bunch of fucking bullshit. And a lot of you dopes buy this shit. I mean, he's good at it, he's smooth, he's selling something that sounds awful nice, and you're really not equipped to judge. All you know is it feels pretty damn good grazing back and forth across your brain. "Reaching out," he says, ooh, "reach out for love," oh yeah!, "loving me is loving each other," ooh, yeah baby.

Bullshit! Columbia Record Club! Twelve records free! Well there is a right and wrong, you fuckers, and it's not a question of reaching out and loving, it's a question of DOING RIGHT. And of NOT DOING WRONG.

IT AIN'T FUCKING COMPLICATED.

Now—

GOD WHO LOVES: Excuse me.

GOD WHO JUDGES: You shutup. Now I—

GOD WHO LOVES: Excuse me, I'm sorry, but—

GOD WHO JUDGES: Hey, who's got the floor!

GOD WHO LOVES: Well I'm sorry, but I cannot just let this pass. Impugning my—

GOD WHO JUDGES: Oh, shut the fuck up!

GOD WHO LOVES: No no! Impugning my motives? You say "Columbia Record Club," as if I'm—

GOD WHO JUDGES: Yeah, with your cheap-shit come-on, trying to rope these boobs in by telling 'em what they want to hear!

GOD WHO LOVES: Now that is *not* the case! You can present a competing point of view, but you *can*not—

GOD WHO JUDGES: Shut. The fuck. Up.

GOD WHO LOVES: No. No no. This is theater of ideas, this is not yelling and screaming. I'm sorry. This is beyond the pale.

GOD WHO JUDGES: Shut your fucking piehole!

GOD WHO LOVES: This is not David Mamet!

GOD WHO JUDGES: Oh, very fucking funny!

GOD WHO LOVES: This is not daytime TV, you know, Jerry Springer. This is the most important debate there is and it is not silly show business and it is *certainly* not about deprecating and—and—and impugning!

GOD WHO JUDGES: It's about telling it like it is, you namby-pamby FUCK!

GOD WHO LOVES: Which does not mean hectoring, my friend. It means laying things out so that these people can choose the God who fulfills their particular needs.

God Who Judges stares at him.

GOD WHO JUDGES: Fulfills their particular needs. Lemme explain something. If I don't fulfill their particular—*(turns to audience)*—If I don't fulfill your particular needs, guess what? *(cups his hands to his mouth)* FUCK! YOU!

GOD WHO LOVES: Well that's just perfect.

GOD WHO JUDGES: Now lemme finish—

GOD WHO LOVES: This is, I think, just a splendid illustration of the limits of a certain kind of theology.

GOD WHO JUDGES: Lemme finish my thing here or you're gonna have a big fucking problem.

GOD WHO LOVES: I *will* let you finish if you adhere to the ground rules. I will let you *finish* if—

GOD WHO JUDGES: A big fucking problem.

GOD WHO LOVES: —if you—look, I'm gonna respect you if you respect me.

GOD WHO JUDGES: Keep it up. You keep it up, and I'm gonna bust your fucking hole.

GOD WHO LOVES: Number one, you don't intimidate me. Number two—

GOD WHO JUDGES: Okay. I warned you. I warned you, right?

GOD WHO LOVES: *(unimpressed)* Yeah, yeah. Number two—

GOD WHO JUDGES: Did I warn you.

GOD WHO LOVES: Yeah, yeah.

GOD WHO JUDGES: Did I fucking warn you.

GOD WHO LOVES: Yeah, look. Number—

God Who Judges punches God Who Loves in the mouth.

GOD WHO LOVES: Ooph!

GOD WHO JUDGES: I fucking warned you! Yes?

He slaps God Who Loves.

GOD WHO LOVES: *(hand pressed to bleeding mouth)* Oh my God!

GOD WHO JUDGES: I've had it with your holier-than-thou SHIT!

He starts kicking God Who Loves in the ass.

GOD WHO JUDGES: Here you go! Faggot!

God Who Loves whirls and slaps ineffectually at God Who Judges.

GOD WHO LOVES: Quit it—kike!

God Who Judges punches God Who Loves again.

GOD WHO JUDGES: Make me, faggot!

God Who Loves runs offstage, weeping:

GOD WHO LOVES: Fucker! Fucker!

GOD WHO JUDGES: Come back here and say that, faggot!

He looks off as we hear God Who Loves's receding sobs. Finally, when they have ebbed to silence, God Who Judges turns back to the audience.

GOD WHO JUDGES: Well, that's that. I've said it before, I'll say it again: these false gods'll fucking kill ya. Now I want you to remember this, how I kicked the shit out of that false fucker. And I want you to lead virtuous lives. And the last thing I w—

BANG!
God Who Judges clutches at his side and staggers, wide-eyed.
God Who Loves runs back in pointing a pistol, laughing maniacally: BANG! BANG!

GOD WHO LOVES: Big man! Heh? How's it feel? Heh? *Heh?!* *Big* shot?

BANG! BANG!
God Who Judges writhes and dies.
Hysterical, eyes flashing, God Who Loves looks out at the audience.

GOD WHO LOVES: Anyone else want a piece a me?

Beat.

GOD WHO LOVES: Yeah! Huh! I thought so.

He nods, smiling sickly.

GOD WHO LOVES: Let's see how you fuckers like it without having God around to wipe your ass for you!

He raises the gun to his temple: BANG!
He falls.
The two bodies, motionless.
A long beat.
Two angels enter in immaculate white robes, with halos, hold-
    ing lyres. They look down at the bodies.
Another long beat.
Finally, still gazing down:

ANGEL ONE: Jesus fuck . . .

Very still.
The lights fade.

* * *

Lights come up on the two angels frozen in the same regard
    but now they are stage right when before they were stage
    left (or vice versa), facing the opposite way, the orienta-
    tion of the dead bodies likewise flipped, the angels' looks
    cheated upstage rather than out to the audience. They are
    standing in hard backlight. The lectern has been spun 180
    degrees to face away from us, as have the two straight-
    backed chairs which now stand to the lectern's other side.

ANGEL ONE: Jesus fuck . . .

Very still.
After the lights fade this time and the actors steal off, lights
    come up beyond on a youngish couple in a row of theater
    seats facing the action. The couple, and the people on either
    side, applaud with no great enthusiasm.
The people on either side rise, gather their belongings, and
    shuffle along the line of seats to depart. The young couple
    lingers.

YOUNG WOMAN: I don't get it.

YOUNG MAN: It was, like, God.

YOUNG WOMAN: Well I know *that*.

YOUNG MAN: Like two Gods. Two ideas of God.

YOUNG WOMAN: Yeah, I know.

YOUNG MAN: *(shrugs)* Well?

They stand.

YOUNG WOMAN: It was just kinda . . . *stupid*.

YOUNG MAN: *(non-commital)* Uh-huh. You want a drink or something?

Blackout.

* * *

Lights come up on the downstage area as a waiter sweeps in, holding high a small table and clutching two menus. The young couple follows him.

The waiter sets the table just downstage of the two straight-backed chairs and then spins the chairs from back-facing to side-on, facing each other across the table, with some cheat out to the audience. He gestures with a flourish and the couple sits.

Meanwhile the lectern is being pushed to one side—still facing away from us—by a maitre d' who then takes up his post behind it. The maitre d' should be, for reasons that will become clear, a strapping young man.

As the scene begins the maitre d' unstows from a shelf inside

*the lectern a large reservations book and phone and mint
salver and small ceramic box holding toothpicks, and
arranges them on the lectern's top. Finished set-dressing,
he awaits arriving guests, fussing with his book. The
lights on him dim slowly so that, once established, he unob-
trusively fades from the scene.*

*The young playgoers have been talking while following the
waiter and waiting for him to plant table and arrange
chairs:*

YOUNG MAN: . . . don't know if it was really supposed to.

YOUNG WOMAN: So you *liked* it?

YOUNG MAN: I don't know, liked it, didn't like it. It was interest-
ing. You didn't like it.

YOUNG WOMAN: It was not my cup of tea.

YOUNG MAN: I'm sorry.

YOUNG WOMAN: No, nothing to apologize for. It was just not
my cup of tea.

YOUNG MAN: Eileen thought we might like it.

YOUNG WOMAN: Eileen?

YOUNG MAN: Yeah.

YOUNG WOMAN: You still talk to Eileen?

YOUNG MAN: Mm-hmm.

YOUNG WOMAN: You still talk to her?

YOUNG MAN: Yeah.

YOUNG WOMAN: Boy. *She* liked it?

YOUNG MAN: Yeah. Eileen likes thought-provoking plays and stuff. We still talk. She recommends books and stuff.

YOUNG WOMAN: Well—I can't believe you said that.

YOUNG MAN: What?

YOUNG WOMAN: "Eileen likes thought-provoking plays." That is so uncool.

YOUNG MAN: Huh?

YOUNG WOMAN: You think I don't like thought-provoking plays? Because I didn't like *that* play? I can't believe you said that. That is so lame.

YOUNG MAN: I didn't *say* that. I didn't say *that*.

YOUNG WOMAN: Like, what, God kicks God in the ass? And then God shoots God? And then God commits suicide? Like that is real thought-provoking. Somebody doesn't find that thought-provoking they're suddenly they're a dumbbell?

YOUNG MAN: I didn't say any of that.

YOUNG WOMAN: And then, like, you compare me to Eileen, which is *so* uncool.

YOUNG MAN: I'm sorry, but I just didn't—

YOUNG WOMAN: Like I don't read books? Maybe I read books. Have you asked me what good books I've read lately? Instead of assuming I'm, like, illiterate? Maybe I read *books* about

God instead of going to stupid shows where God kicks God in the ass.

YOUNG MAN: That is really unfair.

YOUNG WOMAN: Okay, I'll tell you what's unfair: you talking to Eileen about dates you're going on. Do you talk about the dates afterward?

WAITER: Do we know what we want?

YOUNG MAN: No, I—we—need a minute.

YOUNG WOMAN: 'Cause like Eileen used to talk to me about you. I just don't think that's cool.

YOUNG MAN: What do you mean, about me? About *us*? Eileen and me?

YOUNG WOMAN: Believe me, I didn't ask her to. *I* don't want to know about your sexual problems.

YOUNG MAN: What're you talking about?

The woman picks up her menu and studies it.

YOUNG WOMAN: Oh—drop it.

YOUNG MAN: No, what did she say?

YOUNG WOMAN: Oh—just drop it. Do you know what you want?

YOUNG MAN: I don't have sexual problems.

YOUNG WOMAN: Fine. Whatever.

YOUNG MAN: I really don't. I'm not being defensive.

YOUNG WOMAN: Uh-huh. Have you eaten here before?

Blackout on the couple.

* * *

*Lights go up on the maitre d's station. The maitre d', on the
phone, his back to us, leans on his podium with a hand
cupped to his forehead.*

MAITRE D': Because I can't . . . Because I'm going out after . . .
Because . . . I *did* answer; the answer was "Because." . . . I
think it's clear . . . I think it's clear . . . Mm-hmm . . . Well, I
think it's clear . . . Then that's how you feel . . . Then that's
how you feel . . . Look, I know what you're trying to do and it
doesn't affect me . . . It doesn't affect me . . . *(stiffens)* How
many pills? . . . When did y—

*A customer is approaching, shrugging off his overcoat. It is
God Who Judges, now in street clothes, his Old Testament
shock of hair more or less tamed.*

GOD WHO JUDGES: Sternberger. Party of two.

The maitre d' holds up a finger, asking for one second.

MAITRE D': *(into phone)* . . . You did or you're going to? . . . You
did take them? Or you're *going* to? . . .

Beat.

GOD WHO JUDGES: Hello. I'm standing here.

The maitre d' nods vigorously and again holds up one finger.

MAITRE D': *(into phone)* . . . You think I don't know what you're doing? I know what you're doing . . . Look—

GOD WHO JUDGES: I'm standing here.

MAITRE D': Look—hold on. *(presses the handset into his shoulder)* Sorry.

GOD WHO JUDGES: Sternberger. Three E's. Two. Ten-thirty.

MAITRE D': Yes. Let me . . . Sorry . . . *(flips the handset and talks into it, shoulder-wedged, as he opens the reservation book)* You there?

GOD WHO JUDGES: Oh, for fuck's sake!

MAITRE D': Sir, please don't be rude.

GOD WHO JUDGES: *I'm* rude? *I'm* rude?

MAITRE D: Sir, I'm helping you—

GOD WHO JUDGES: You're chatting on your fucking phone there. You've got *one* customer and a fucking half-empty restaurant—*(breaks off, gazing into the audience)* . . . Never mind, I see my friend. *(muttered, leaving)* Prick.

MAITRE D': *(muttered)* Asshole . . . *(into phone, teeth grit)* All right. You know how you're making me feel? You know how you're making me feel? Like I'm gonna hit someone, so help me God. You're gonna make me haul off and— . . . I *never* said that, *never*! . . . Great, good for you, you do whatever you're gonna do, ya know?—that's fucking *great*! Fuck. *Look.* I'm at work. Don't make me yell. Don't make me do this. *LOOK.*

Blackout.

* * *

*Lights come up on the restaurant table. It is now occupied not
by the young couple but by a lone woman peering into a
compact mirror. God Who Judges, whom given our new
perspective we shall henceforth call Actor, enters. His lady
friend snaps her compact shut and greets him with a lip-
to-lip peck.*

LADY FRIEND: Hi.

ACTOR: Hi.

He sits.

LADY FRIEND: How was the show?

ACTOR: Yeah. It was okay. Well—it was off, actually.

LADY FRIEND: Oh yeah? How so?

ACTOR: A little stiff. First three rows were all priests. Church
group. It threw me.

LADY FRIEND: Uh.

ACTOR: They shouldn't book 'em in a block like that. All up
front. Jesus Christ. Or at least warn the actors.

LADY FRIEND: Uh-huh.

ACTOR: Jesus, it's like, you know, uh, having Hugh Hefner come
over and watch you screw.

LADY FRIEND: An expert.

ACTOR: Yeah. How is it not gonna make you uptight.

LADY FRIEND: Uh-huh.

ACTOR: Fucking priests. Man, I was just busting the, what, the greeter-guy, the host, I was just busting his agates there, just from being pissed off about the show.

LADY FRIEND: Huh.

ACTOR: Boy. *No*body laughed when I kicked Jerry in the ass.

LADY FRIEND: Uh-huh.

ACTOR: Like, *no*body.

LADY FRIEND: Well . . .

ACTOR: Well what?

LADY FRIEND: Oh—we don't have to get into it.

ACTOR: No; what? God kicking God in the ass? That isn't funny?

LADY FRIEND: Uh-huh.

ACTOR: Gets a *hearty* laugh.

LADY FRIEND: Uh-huh.

ACTOR: Usually.

LADY FRIEND: Fine. I told you: it doesn't work for women.

ACTOR: Doesn't work for—what does men-women have to do with it? God kicking God in the ass?!

LADY FRIEND: Fine. So, the priests laughed?

ACTOR: No! *Fuck* no!

LADY FRIEND: So it's *not* just women.

ACTOR: It's—*you* said it was men-women! *I* don't think it's men-women!

LADY FRIEND: *(sighs)* Okay, fine Dan. Let's not talk about it.

ACTOR: Fine! Fine. *(examines the menu)*

LADY FRIEND: I just think it's a silly play.

He puts down his menu and stares.

ACTOR: . . . That's not talking about it?

LADY FRIEND: What.

ACTOR: "It's a silly play"—that's not talking about it? The play?

LADY FRIEND: Well, I thought you'd want me to be honest. Excuse me. Now I know.

ACTOR: Know what?

LADY FRIEND: You just want praise. Fine. That's okay. That's the sense I always get from you. That you just want reinforcement, fine, but at least let's be honest about *that*.

ACTOR: What the fuck? What're you, studying jujitsu?

LADY FRIEND: What're you talking about? What's the import of *that* witticism, Dan?

ACTOR: First we're not gonna talk about it, you suggest we don't talk about the play, okay, so fine, and then another little dig, "it's a silly play." And then, I mean before that, you say there's a gender thing behind how people react to the play, that it's men-women, and then all of a sudden I'm some incorrect *dolt* because you think *I* made some gender distinction. Which I didn't even.

LADY FRIEND: Okay, fine, whatever, but instead of obsessing about *that*, Dan, which who cares, why don't we try to be honest about *you*. About how everything has to be *your* way, you always know everything. There's no such thing as honest disagreement.

ACTOR: *(martyred)* What did I say. What the FUCK did I say. I just want a nice meal, relax after the show, have a good time—

LADY FRIEND: *(finger-quotes)* "A good time." *Praise* is what you want. Let's not talk about our *feelings* is what you want. Let's not engage. Let's just have a "good time."

ACTOR: Jesus fucking Christ on a stick. You know, your problem is you didn't fucking *understand* the play. You should see it again. *(she hoots)* I'm serious. And not because I give a shit if you like what *I* do; you just didn't fucking *get* it. Or you wouldn't give me this kind of shit.

LADY FRIEND: Well Dan, you've lost me. If our talking about our feelings is me giving you shit, which I don't accept the premise, but whatever you want to call it, I'm sorry if I'm treading on eggshells here, call it man-woman stuff or *not* man-woman who *gives* a shit, if gender is a minefield for you, okay, fine, but what does it have to do with your *play?* Your stupid *play* is about *God.*

ACTOR: The play is not about *one* thing!

LADY FRIEND: Dan. Honey.

ACTOR: See, this is a mistake you make—

LADY FRIEND: Dan. Listen to me. I love you. The play. Is fucking. Inane.

ACTOR: No.

LADY FRIEND: Schtick.

ACTOR: No. No. You should understand it maybe before you dismiss it. Honey-bunch.

LADY FRIEND: Dan. Okay, fine. The play is a masterpiece. All its patriarchal assumptions I thought were just almost unbelievably penetrating. But I'm just a woman and I guess some of it went over my head, I guess the part where you kick Jerry in the ass, just, the subtleties of the issues raised by that got by me. So let me approach it in a different way, Dan. Dan: I don't give a shit about your work.

ACTOR: I'm not talking about my *work!* It's not *me!* The *issues* are relevant! All of your "feelings" shit! Who gives a fuck! We live, we eat, we shit, we fuck! Like the nomad Hebrews in the Middle East three thousand fucking years ago! Who made feelings king? Feelings are fucking bullshit! Feelings are the fruity little bow on the box! Who put feelings centerstage, man—some *woman?* When did we get down on our knees to our fucking FEELINGS?

Blackout.

* * *

In black, a voice:

YOUNG WOMAN: I just think all the ideas were kind of phony. You know. It was just stick figures up there preaching. Like, *literally.*

The lights come up to show that the table is once again occupied by the young couple. In this scene change, and in the next two as well, the opening speech in black should cover the actors' traffic so that the new scene's dialogue butts up against the old.

YOUNG MAN: Uh-huh.

YOUNG WOMAN: A good play has characters, you know, real people, or they *could* be real. I mean if the play just lays out ideas without bothering to put them in the mouth of real characters, then it's just like pretentious.

YOUNG MAN: Okay. Good. I see that. That's a good point. So what did Eileen say about me?

YOUNG WOMAN: Oh, you know what? Forget about that. I mean if the ideas, you know—

YOUNG MAN: There was like *one night* when we were really drunk—

YOUNG WOMAN: —if it's not people *having* the ideas, then who cares? Ideas aren't, you know. You have to connect them to *people.* It has to be *grounded.*

YOUNG MAN: *(impatient)* Yeah yeah, I *get* it. Boy, you know. Eileen is, like—

YOUNG WOMAN: That's just lazy if you don't. That's called lazy writing.

WAITER: Do we know what we want?

YOUNG MAN: Ummm . . . Could, um . . .

YOUNG WOMAN: 'Cause otherwise, you know . . . Could I have the Cobb salad?

YOUNG MAN: I, um . . . I need a minute.

YOUNG WOMAN: You can't even say, like, this actor was good or that one was really good, because there weren't even characters. It was just a bunch of lecturing.

YOUNG MAN: Well it wasn't *just* lecturing. There was God kicking God in the ass.

YOUNG WOMAN: That didn't work for me.

Blackout.

* * *

In black until indicated.

LADY FRIEND: You fuck me in the pussy, Dan! You never fuck me in the *heart*! You never fuck me in the *head*! I feel mounted and violated! *(lights up)* Mounted and violated! You fuck my pussy, Dan! You are a shallow, shallow pussy-fucker!

WAITER: *(entering)* Madam, sir, could you please—

ACTOR: I don't know what you're talking about! *You* don't know what you're talking about! You're talking *bull*shit!

LADY FRIEND: Why no children, Dan?! Why have you NEVER had a STABLE! LONGLASTING! RELATIONSHIP!

ACTOR: Goddamnit! GODDAMNIT!

WAITER: Sir—

LADY FRIEND: YOU CANNOT RELATE TO PEOPLE IN A NORMAL WAY! WHY IS THAT, DAN?!

ACTOR: ALL RIGHT!

WAITER: Madam—

LADY FRIEND: YOU THINK YOUR FEELINGS DON'T AFFECT HOW YOU *BEHAVE*?!

ACTOR: GOD FUCKIT!

Blackout.

* * *

In black until indicated:

YOUNG MAN: I thought the actors *were* good. Like the angry guy.

YOUNG WOMAN: How can you *say* that? He was, like, yelling. How can he be good if it's just yelling. *(lights up)* It was all meaningless. It was all stuff that wasn't real, it wasn't the real world. That's why, you know, even though it was all trying to be all deep, it just ends up . . . *(stares)* Oh my God. Oh my God, don't look. It's God.

Young Man: . . . What?

Young Woman: It's the God guy. Over there. At that table.—
Don't turn around! It's the God guy. The God actor guy. The
God yelling God guy.—Don't look!

Young Man: He was good.

Young Woman: Oh my God. He's yelling at the woman he's
with.—Don't! Just act natural!

Young Man: I am!

Young Woman: —Oh my God, I can't believe he's just sitting
here having dinner, arguing!

Young Man: Well, actors have to eat too.

Young Woman: I can't believe you *said* that! Like I'm some
hick who's never seen an actor!

Young Man: I didn't say that!

Young Woman: I don't even think he's a *good* actor!

Young Man: Well you're the one who made the big deal!

Young Woman: I didn't say it was a big deal! I know that actors
have to eat! Like what, they're not gonna eat! I can't believe
you said that to me!

Young Man: Look, I didn't say—It was just innocent—

Young Woman: —God's getting up! Boy, they're really going at
it. The greeter-guy, um, host is running over. Oh my God!—
Don't look! Will you please be cool? He's shoving! God is

shoving the greeter-guy—oh God! The greeter just—punched God! The greeter is . . . He's KICKING GOD IN THE ASS! THE GREETER-GUY IS KICKING GOD IN THE ASS! HE'S—

The young man finally turns and looks. Both he and the woman stare. After a long beat, their reactions sync as the beating apparently escalates:

YOUNG MAN AND WOMAN: Oh! . . . OH! . . . *OH!*

Blackout.

* * *

A long beat, and then, in blackness, a blandly neutral voice, amplified:

VOICE: Welcome to "The Debate." The powers that be have asked that we turn off our cell phones and pagers, and please also unwrap any crinkly crackly candies before the show begins. And, finally, please note that in tonight's performance the role of God Who Judges, normally played by Daniel Sternberger, is being played by John J. MacDonald.

Long silence.
A new voice:

VOICE: What do we call it?

Lights come up on the familiar bare-bones set of lectern and straightbacked chairs, upon one of which sits waiting God Who Loves. Behind the lectern stands a new God Who Judges, not an imposing person; his lank and receding hair compares poorly with the original's powerful shock of white. Wardrobe and words may be the same and the actor

is not terrible, but he cannot muster the effortless authority
of the first God Who Judges. He is, after all, only the un-
derstudy.

UNDERSTUDY: What do we call it? What do we call it? Anyone?
What do we call it we call it the Ten Commandments. Okay?
Not the Ten fucking Suggestions. They are a fucking moral
imperative, you miserable sacks of shit. Now I want to see
this shit *observed.*

The lights begin to fade. Just before they reach full black the
understudy summons a halfhearted:

UNDERSTUDY: Fuckers!